Sally

Lehrwerk für den
Englischunterricht ab Klasse 1

Sally's English Test 1/2
Lernstandskontrollen

Erarbeitet von
Jasmin Brune
Daniela Elsner
Stefanie Gleixner-Weyrauch
Marion Lugauer
Sabine Schwarz

Unter Beratung von Jane Brockmann-Fairchild

Illustriert von
Barbara Jung
Wilfried Poll
Thilo Pustlauk

Oldenbourg Schulbuchverlag, München

Redaktion: Bea Herrmann
Illustration: Susanne Bochem, Christine Brand, Barbara Jung, Monica May, Wilfried Poll, Thilo Pustlauk
Umschlagkonzept: Mendell & Oberer, München
Umschlaggestaltung: Renate Möller, Berlin
Umschlagillustration: Wilfried Poll
Layout und technische Umsetzung: MedienDesign Bruggberger

www.oldenbourg.de

1. Auflage, 1. Druck 2016

Alle Drucke dieser Auflage sind inhaltlich unverändert und können im Unterricht nebeneinander verwendet werden.

© 2016 Cornelsen Schulverlage GmbH, Berlin

Das Werk und seine Teile sind urheberrechtlich geschützt.
Jede Nutzung in anderen als den gesetzlich zugelassenen Fällen bedarf der
vorherigen schriftlichen Einwilligung des Verlages.
Hinweis zu den §§ 46, 52a UrhG: Weder das Werk noch seine Teile dürfen
ohne eine solche Einwilligung eingescannt und in ein Netzwerk eingestellt
oder sonst öffentlich zugänglich gemacht werden.
Dies gilt auch für Intranets von Schulen und sonstigen Bildungseinrichtungen.

Druck: H. Heenemann, Berlin

ISBN 978-3-637-02258-4

 Inhalt gedruckt auf säurefreiem Papier, umweltschonend hergestellt aus chlorfrei gebleichten Faserstoffen.

Inhaltsverzeichnis

Vorwort 4

Testbögen Klasse 1

Colours and numbers 5

My schoolbag 6

Body and feelings 7

Toys 8

Clothes (nur Baden-Württemberg) 9

Animals 10

Fruit 11

Family 12

Lösungen Klasse 1 13

Testbögen Klasse 2

At school 15

Body and clothes/I'm Jumping Jack 16

Hobbies 18

Vegetables 20

Weather 22

Farm animals 24

Seasons 26

Lösungen Klasse 2 28

Texte zu den Hörverstehensaufgaben: Sally's English Test 1 32

Texte zu den Hörverstehensaufgaben: Sally's English Test 2 34

Lernstandsbogen 36

Hinweise zur Überprüfung der Sprechfertigkeit 37

Sprachstandsbogen 38

Bildkarten

Vorwort

Das Lehrwerk *Sally* zielt auf eine behutsame Entwicklung der fremdsprachlichen Handlungsfähigkeit. Dabei werden in jeder *unit* alle Teilkompetenzen sukzessiv erweitert. Um zu überprüfen, ob die Schüler ihr fremdsprachliches Wissen und Können weiterentwickelt haben, bietet *Sally's English Test* eine verlässliche Evaluationsmöglichkeit. Die Überprüfung des individuellen Sprachstands eröffnet zum einen der Lehrkraft die Möglichkeit, gegebenenfalls Maßnahmen zur individuellen Förderung treffen zu können. Zum anderen dient eine regelmäßige Feststellung des Leistungsstands als seriöse Grundlage für die in manchen Bundesländern obligatorische Bewertung durch Ziffernnoten. Darüber hinaus werden Eltern und Schüler über den jeweiligen Leistungsfortschritt informiert.

Die Tests

Zu jeder grundlegenden *unit* bietet *Sally's English Test* jeweils einen Testbogen, der das Hörverstehen und den Wortschatz der Lerner überprüft. Ab Klasse 2 werden die Tests durch Aufgaben zur Überprüfung der Lese- und Schreibfähigkeiten ergänzt.
Vor der Bearbeitung der Testbögen sollte die Lehrkraft die Arbeitsaufträge mit den Kindern besprechen:

 ankreuzen, einkreisen, nummerieren, Linien ziehen, schreiben

 malen, anmalen

Es bietet sich an, die Kinder darauf hinzuweisen, dass sie bei einem *colour dictation* zunächst die jeweilige Stelle nur mit einem Strich in der entsprechenden Farbe kennzeichnen und anschließend ausmalen. Der Hörtext wird dabei dreimal abgespielt: hören – malen – überprüfen und berichtigen. Zu jedem Testbogen wird eine Lösungsseite angeboten.
Die Kinder können zur Selbstevaluation auf jedem Bogen ankreuzen, wie sie den Test fanden: leicht (Sally mit leichtem Säckchen), mittel (Sally mit mittelschwerem Säckchen) oder schwierig (Sally mit schwerem Säckchen).

Texte zu den Hörverstehensaufgaben

 Die Hörverstehensaufgaben sind mit einem CD-Symbol gekennzeichnet. Sie befinden sich auf der beiliegenden CD (Audiofassung) sowie auf den Seiten 32 bis 35 (Textfassung).

Bewertung

Zur Vereinheitlichung der Bewertung wurden die Tests so konzipiert, dass für jede Einzelaufgabe 1 Punkt (in Einzelfällen 0,5 Punkte) oder auch 2 Punkte bei besonders anspruchsvollen Aufgaben vergeben werden können. Gegebenenfalls kann pro Fehler 1 Punkt abgezogen werden.
Bitte bedenken Sie, dass die Feststellung der Schülerleistungen durch *Sally's English Test* nur einen Teil der sprachlichen Fertigkeiten der Kinder abdecken kann und daher nur anteilig in die Gesamtbewertung eingehen darf. Einen nicht unerheblichen Teil machen daneben die mündlichen Leistungen der Schüler aus. Zur Überprüfung der Sprechfertigkeit werden vier Bildkarten mit komplexen Bildsituationen angeboten, die jeweils *unit*- und themenübergreifend eingesetzt und dokumentiert werden können (siehe Seite 37 bis 39). Als Hilfe bei der Dokumentation des gesamten Leistungsspektrums steht Ihnen ein Lernstandsbogen zur Verfügung (siehe Seite 36).

Name: Date:

Colours and numbers

 1. Listen and colour. ___/5 Punkte

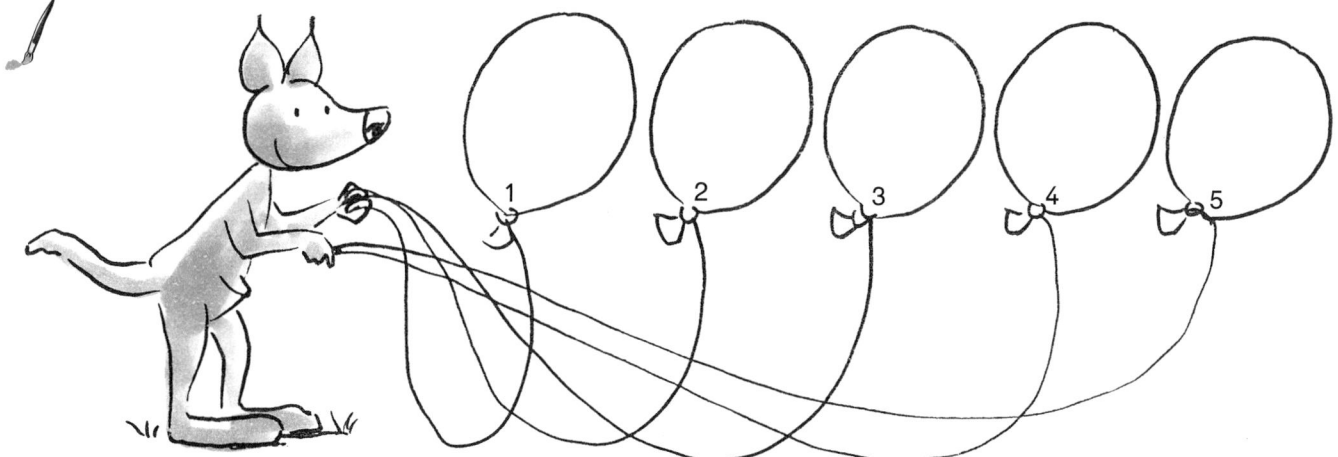

 2. Listen and write the numbers. ___/5 Punkte

 3. Listen and colour. ___/3 Punkte

 Du hast ____ von 13 Punkten erreicht.

Name: Date:

 My schoolbag

1. Listen and draw lines. ___/4 Punkte

2. Listen and colour. ___/3 Punkte

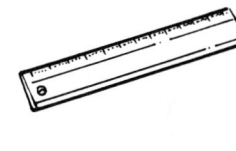  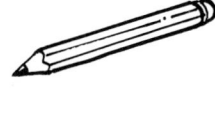  

3. Listen and circle ○. ___/4 Punkte

 Du hast ___ von 11 Punkten erreicht.

Name: _____ Date: _____

 Body and feelings

 1. Listen and circle ○. ___/4 Punkte

 2. Listen and number. ___/4 Punkte

☐ ☐ ☐ ☐

 3. Listen and draw. ___/2 Punkte

 Du hast _____ von 10 Punkten erreicht.

Name: _____ Date: _____

 Toys

1. Listen and colour. ___/5 Punkte

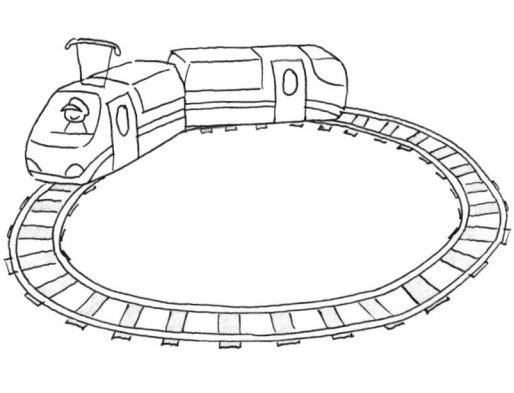

2. Listen and circle ◯ . ___/4 Punkte

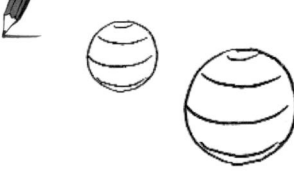

3. Listen and draw. ___/2 Punkte

Du hast _____ von 11 Punkten erreicht.

Name: _____ Date: _____

 **Clothes**

1. **Listen and draw lines.** 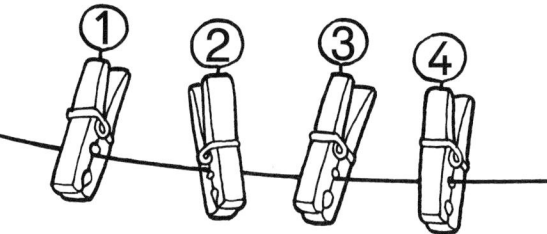 ___/4 Punkte

2. **Find Ellen and Peter. Listen and tick ✓.** ___/4 Punkte

3. **Listen and draw.** ___/3 Punkte

 Du hast _____ von 11 Punkten erreicht.

Name: _____ Date: _____

 Animals

 1. Listen and colour. ___/5 Punkte

 2. Listen and tick ✓. ___/5 Punkte

 3. Listen and draw lines. ___/4 Punkte

①
②
③
④

 Du hast ____ von 14 Punkten erreicht.

Name: _____ Date: _____

 Fruit

 1. Listen and draw. ___/3 Punkte

 2. Listen and circle ○. ___/4 Punkte

 3. Listen and number. ___/4 Punkte

Du hast _____ von 11 Punkten erreicht.

Name: Date:

 Family

1. Listen and number. ___/4 Punkte

2. Listen and draw lines. ___/5 Punkte

3. Listen and colour. ___/3 Punkte

 Du hast _____ von 12 Punkten erreicht.

Lösungen Klasse 1

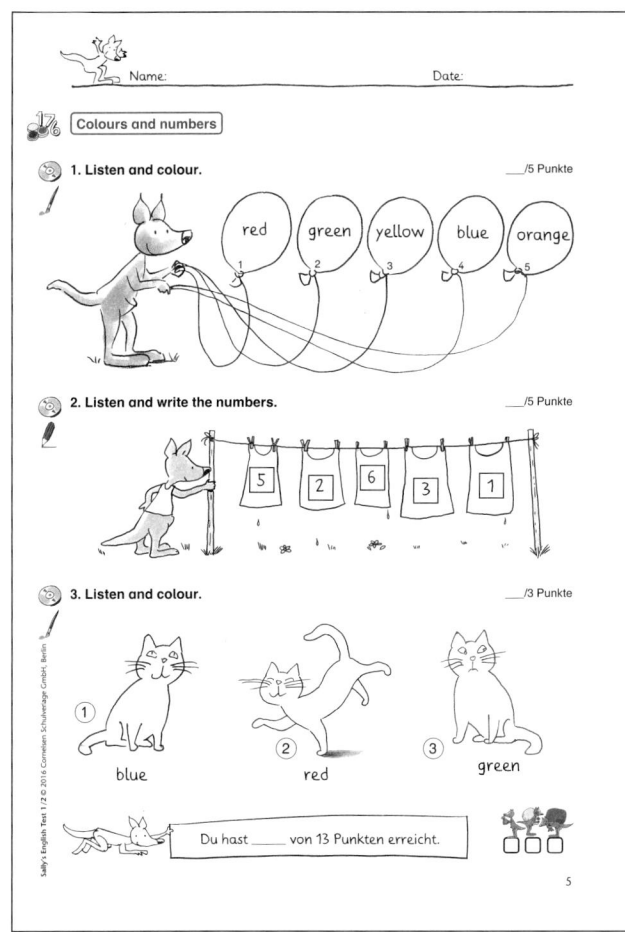
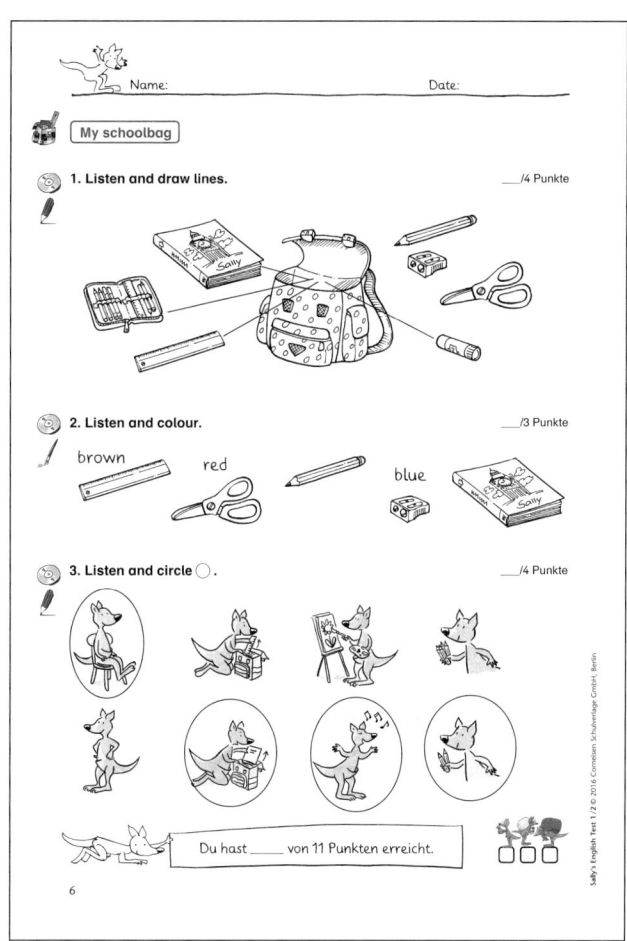
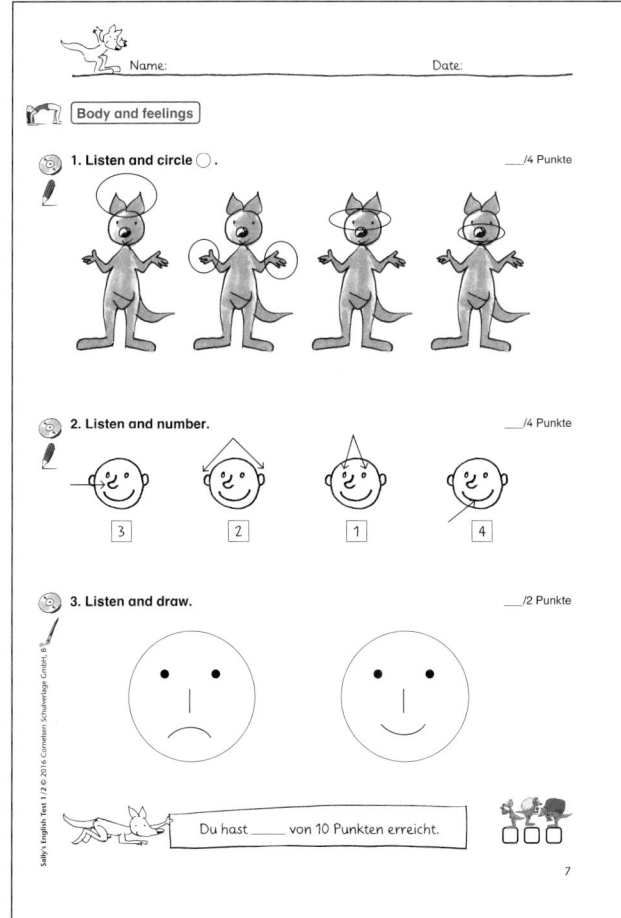
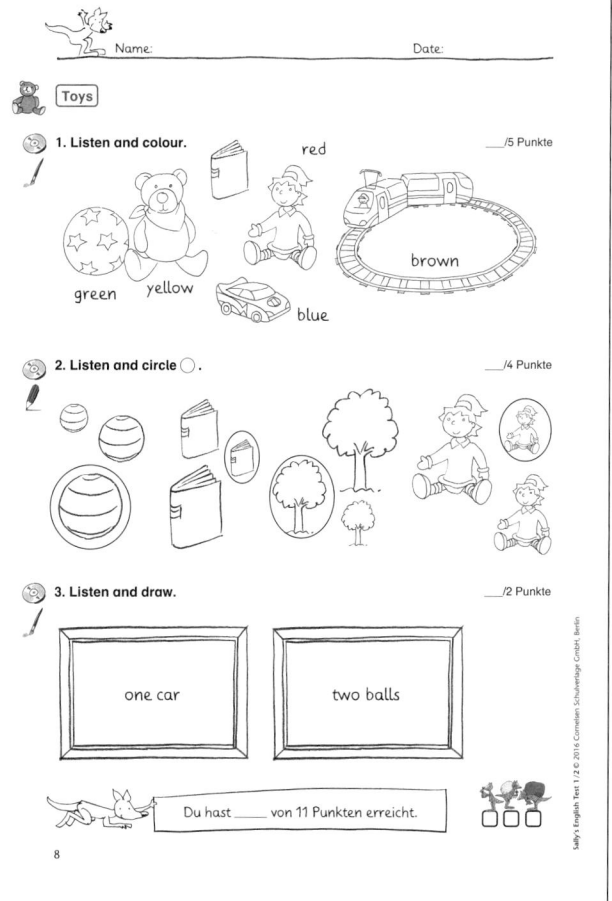

Lösungen Klasse 1

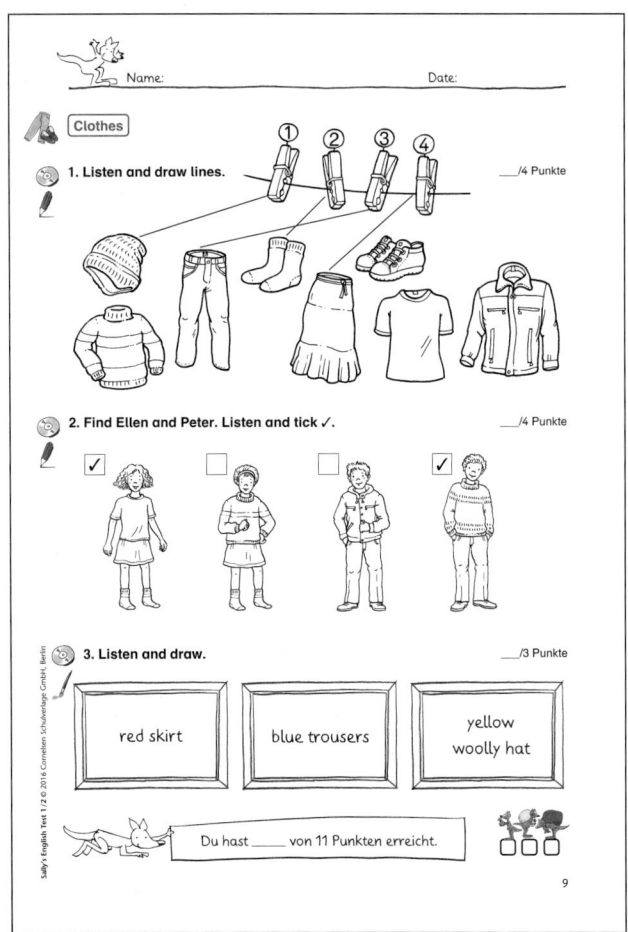

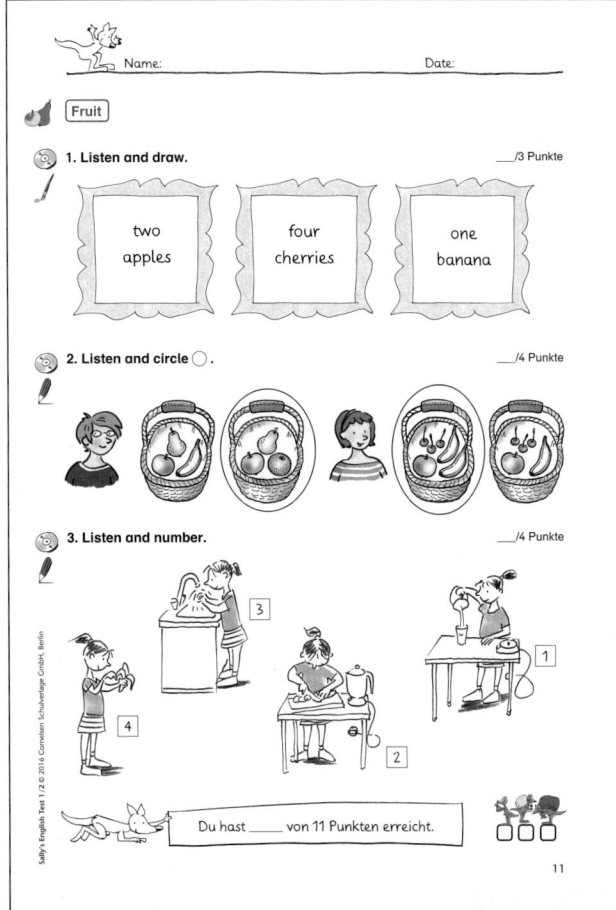

Name: _____ Date: _____

 At school

1. Listen and tick. ___/4 Punkte

2. Listen and write the numbers. ___/4 Punkte

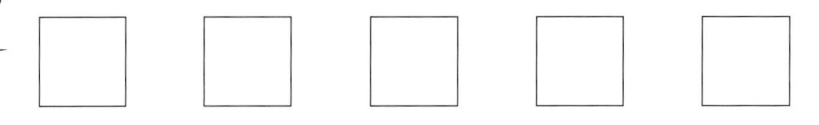

3. Read and write. ___/3 Punkte

pencil case

book

schoolbag

_____ _____ _____

 Du hast _____ von 11 Punkten erreicht.

15

Name: Date:

 **Body and clothes/I'm Jumping Jack**

🔊 **1. Listen and draw lines.** ___/4 Punkte

✏️

    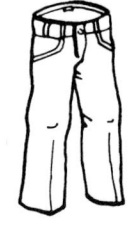

🔊 **2. Listen and number.** ___/4 Punkte

✏️

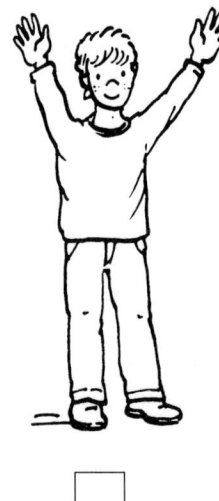   

3. Read and write. ___/4 Punkte

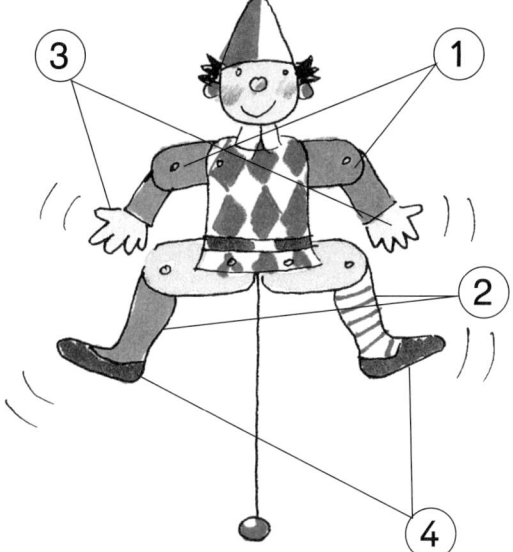

1) 2 _____

2) 2 _____

3) 2 _____

4) 2 _____

feet	arms	hands
legs	shoes	T-shirt
skirt	trousers	

4. Read and write. ___/4 Punkte

_____

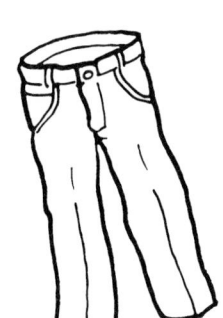

_____

_____

_____

 Du hast _____ von 16 Punkten erreicht.

Name: _____   Date: _____

 Hobbies

 **1. Listen and number.** ___/6 Punkte

 2. Listen and colour. ___/5 Punkte

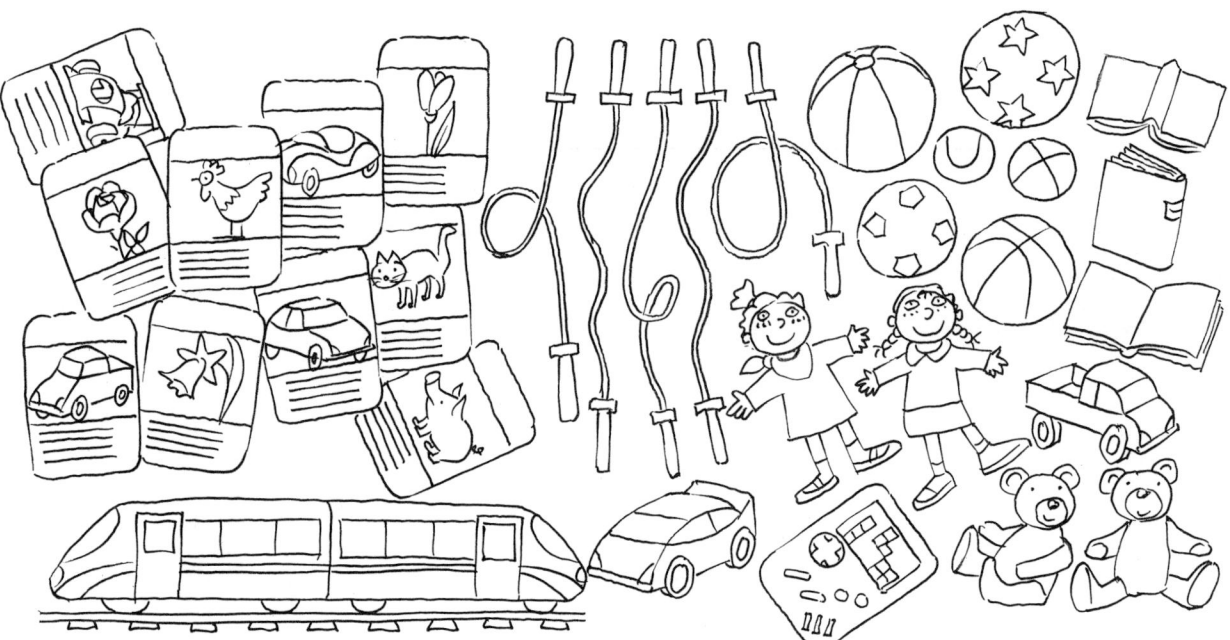

 3. Listen and draw. ___/3 Punkte

4. Read and write. ___/5 Punkte

| ball | gameboy | stickers |
| glue stick | inline skates | playing cards | ruler |

_____

_____

_____

_____

_____

5. Odd one out. ___/2 Punkte

| ball | gameboy | banana |

| stickers | pencil | inline skates |

 Du hast _____ von 21 Punkten erreicht.

Name: Date:

 Vegetables

 1. Listen and draw lines. ___/6 Punkte

 2. Listen and number. ___/4 Punkte

3. Draw lines. ___/6 Punkte

carrot   tomato   cucumber   beans   radishes   lettuce

 4. Find the words. Circle and write. ___/4 Punkte

lettucefhcarrotwvzcucumberqprbean

_____

_____

_____

_____

 Du hast ____ von 20 Punkten erreicht.

 Name: Date:

 Weather

1. Listen and draw lines. ___/4 Punkte

  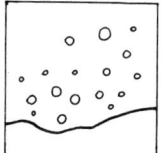 

2. Listen and number. ___/4 Punkte

3. Read and write. ___/4 Punkte

It's _____ .

It's _____ .

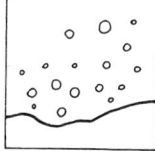 
It's _____ .

It's _____ .

| windy | rainy | snowy | sunny |

4. Find the four weather words. Circle ◯. ___/4 Punkte

f	r	k	o	m	m
e	a	b	s	s	s
w	i	n	d	y	n
w	n	l	t	r	o
u	y	e	b	e	w
i	s	u	n	n	y

 Du hast ____ von 16 Punkten erreicht.

Name: _____ Date: _____

 Farm animals

 1. Listen and number. ___/4 Punkte

 2. Listen and colour. ___/5 Punkte

3. Read and write. ___/7 Punkte

| sheep | goose | cow | duck |
| hen | cat | pig | dog | horse |

4. Find the six farm animals. Circle ◯. ___/6 Punkte

hen   ruler

cow   carrot   pencil   lettuce

ball   shoes   pig   book

skirt   rubber   duck   sheep

cucumber   horse   rope   socks

Du hast ____ von 22 Punkten erreicht.

Name: Date:

 Seasons

 1. Listen and draw lines. ___/8 Punkte

 Emma
 Tom
 Linda
 Bill

 spring
 summer
 autumn
 winter

 2. Listen and tick ✓. ___/6 Punkte

3. Find the season. Write.   ___/3 Punkte

Halloween is in _____ .

Christmas is in _____ .

Easter is in _____ .

4. What's the weather like? Read and write.   ___/4 Punkte

In winter it's _____.

In summer it's _____.

In spring it's _____.

In autumn it's _____.

| snowy | sunny | orange | windy | blue | rainy |

Du hast _____ von 21 Punkten erreicht.

Lösungen Klasse 2

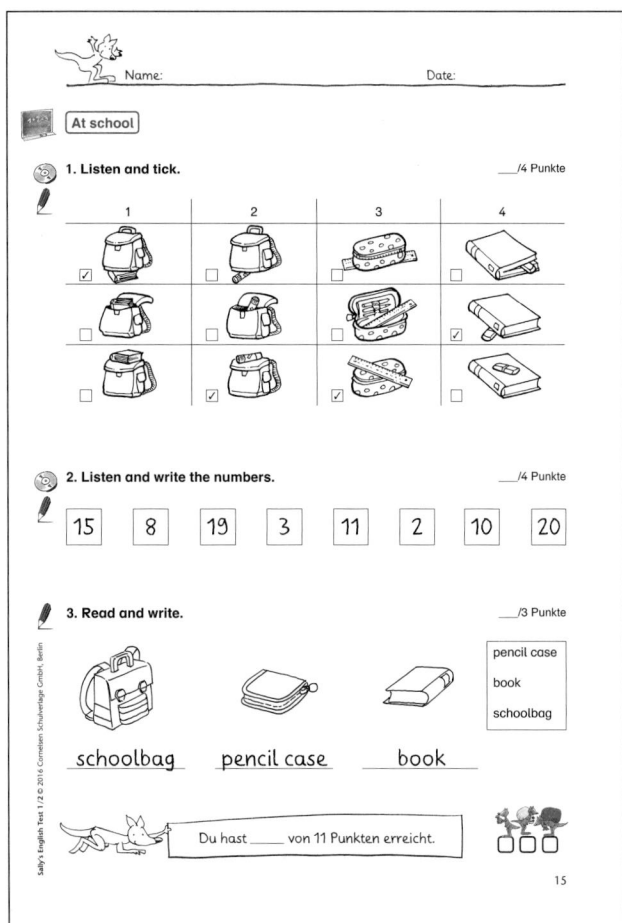
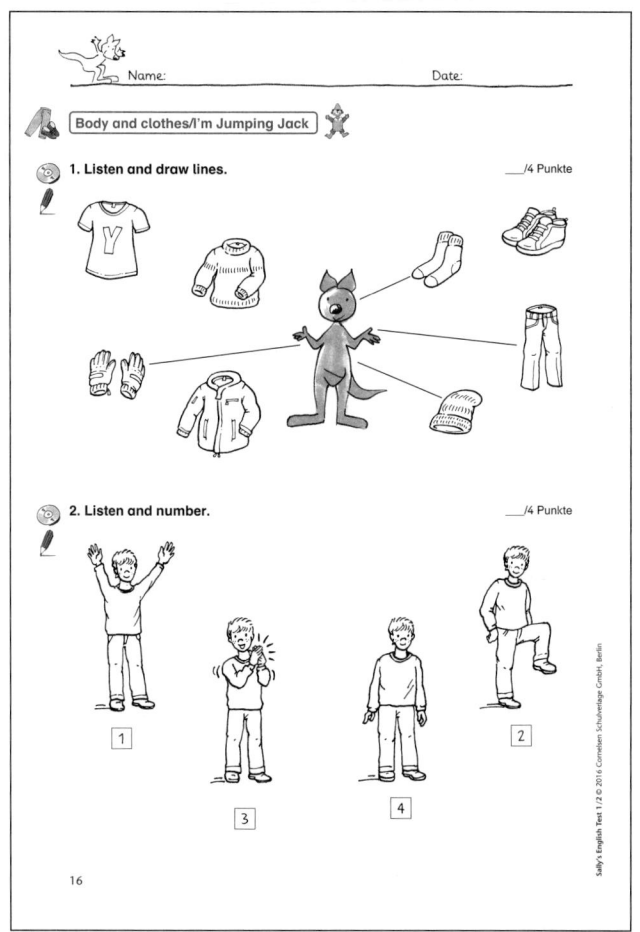
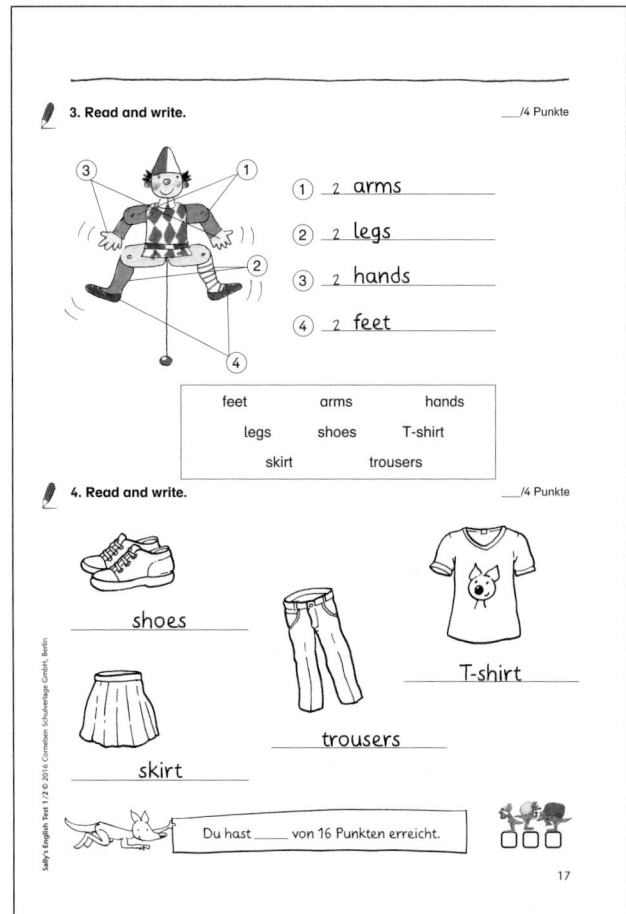
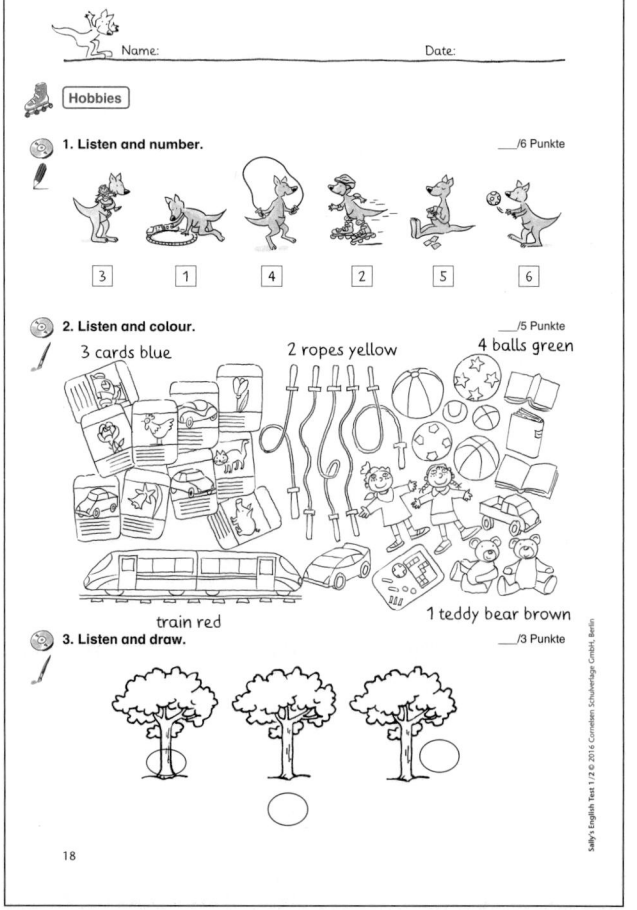

Lösungen Klasse 2

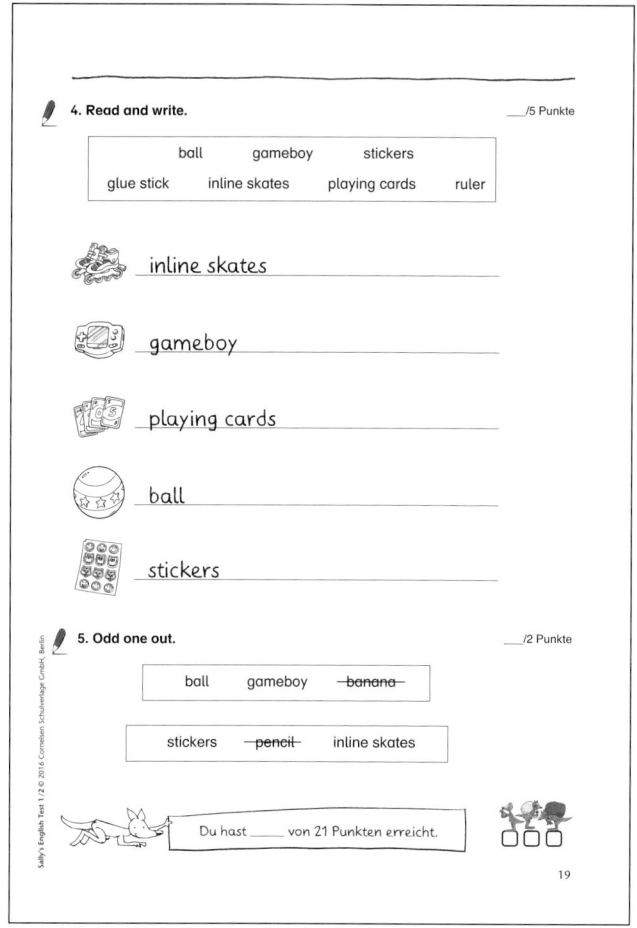

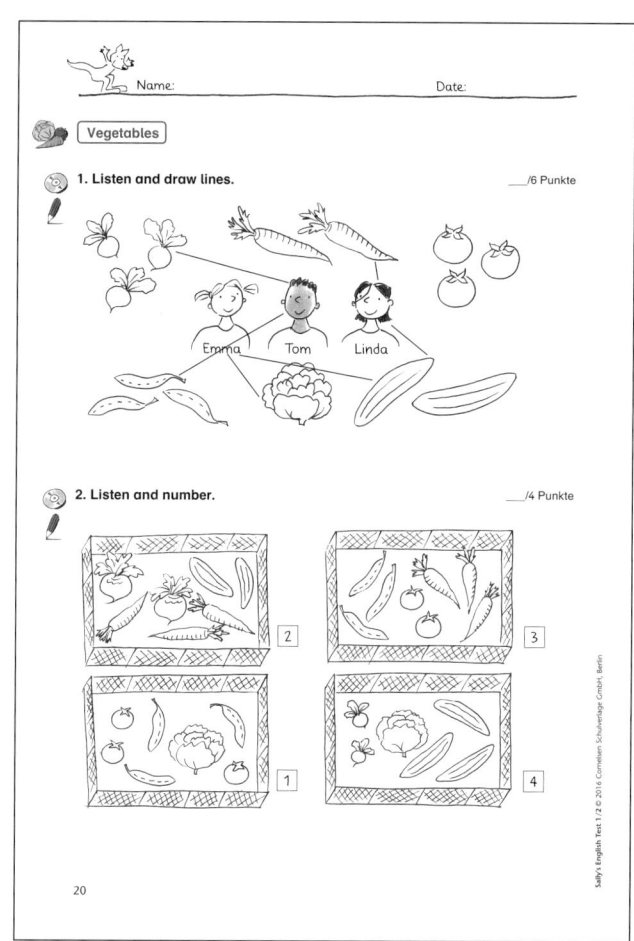

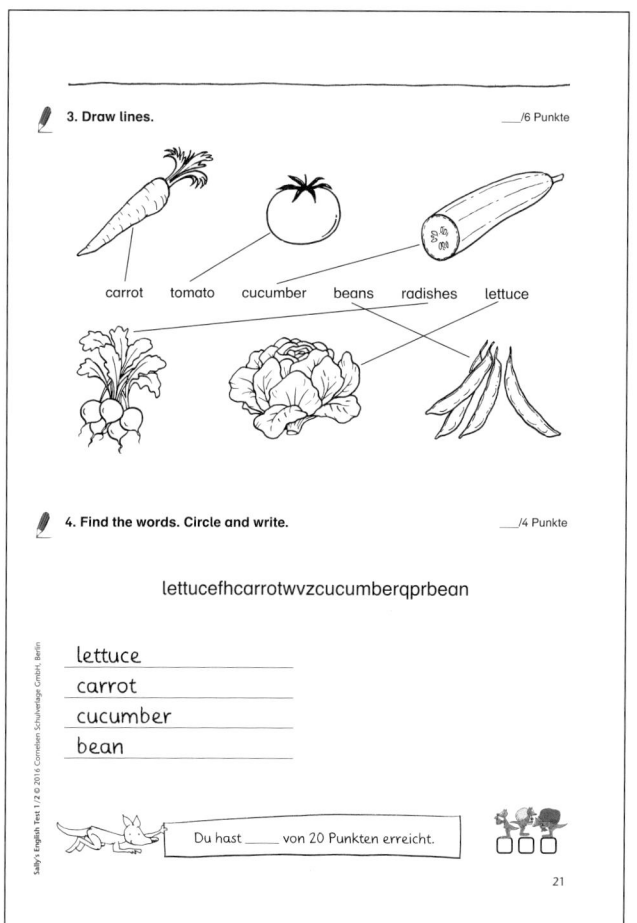

Lösungen Klasse 2

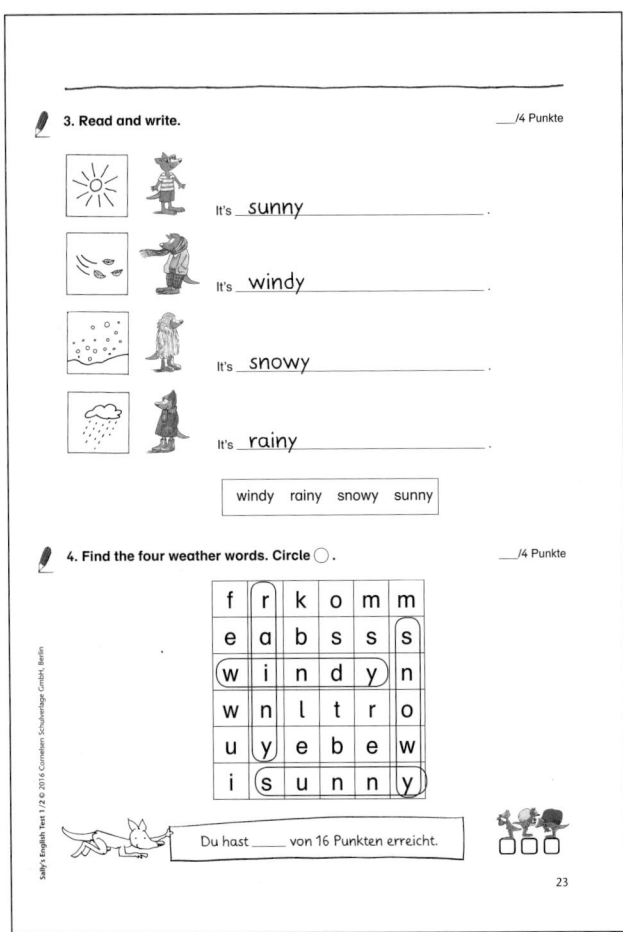

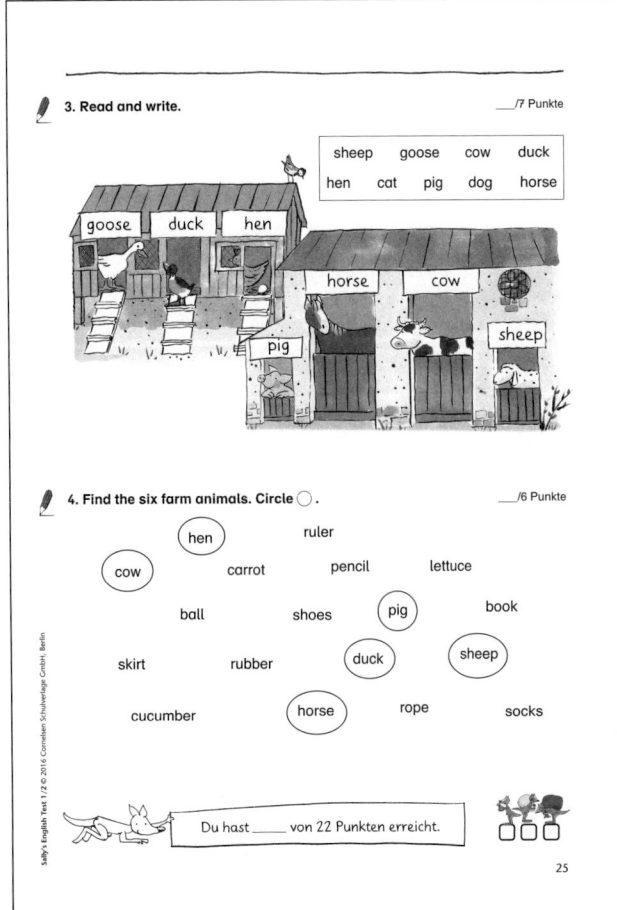

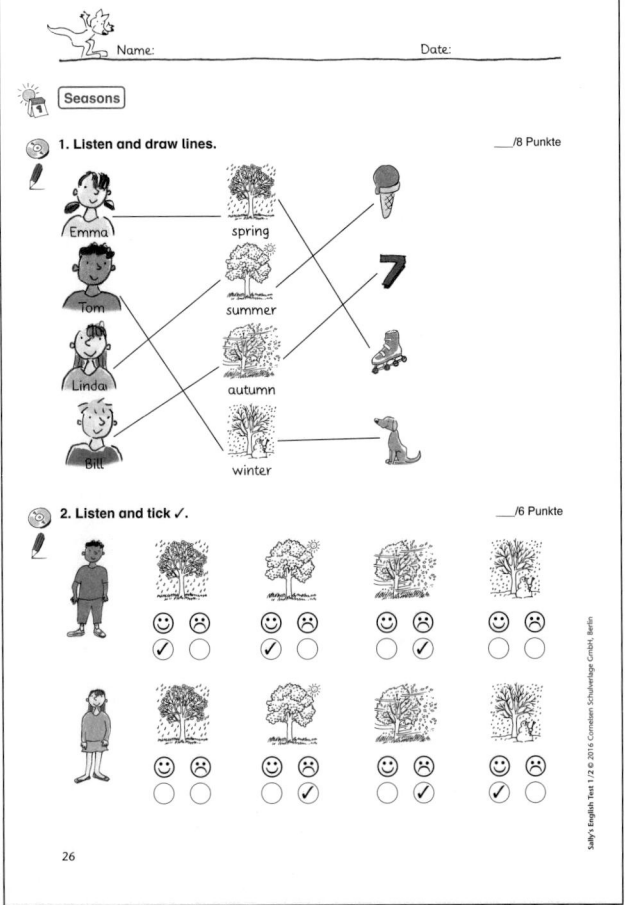

Lösungen Klasse 2

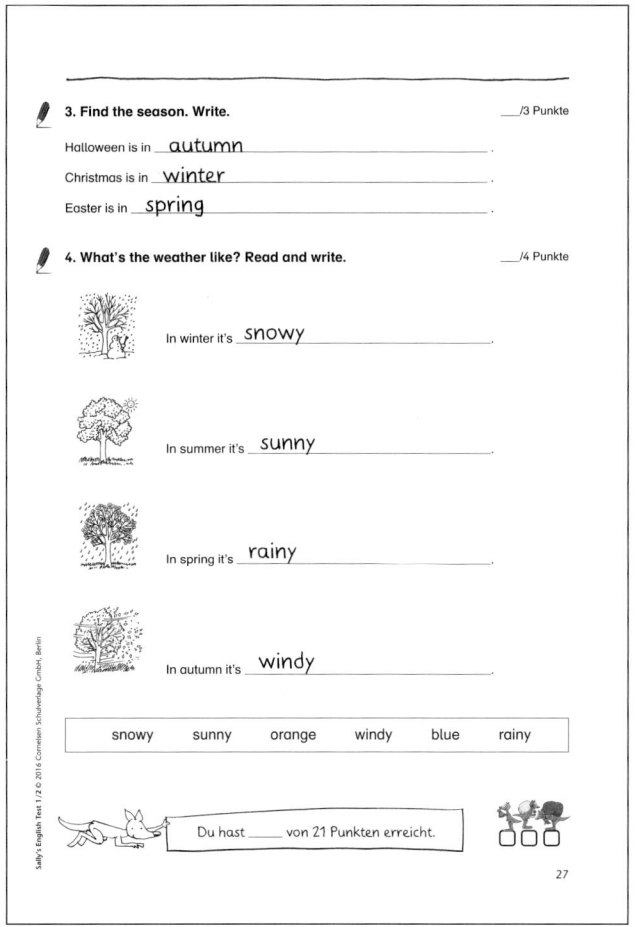

Sally's English Test 1
Texte zu den Hörverstehensaufgaben

Colours and numbers (S. 5)
Zu 1.:
Balloon number 1 is red.
Balloon number 2 is green.
Balloon number 3 is yellow.
Balloon number 4 is blue.
Balloon number 5 is orange.

Zu 2.:
5 – 2 – 6 – 3 – 1

Zu 3.:
Number 1: *"I'm Scat the cat.
I change my colour like that."*
So Scat the cat changes into a blue cat.
Number 2: *"I'm Scat the cat.
I change my colour like that."*
So Scat the cat changes into a red cat.
Number 3: *"I'm Scat the cat.
I change my colour like that."*
So Scat the cat changes into a green cat.

My schoolbag (S. 6)
Zu 1.:
Put the pencil case into the schoolbag.
Now put the book into the schoolbag.
Put the ruler into the schoolbag.
Now put the glue stick into the schoolbag.

Zu 2.:
Colour the ruler brown.
Colour the scissors red.
Colour the pencil sharpener blue.

Zu 3.:
Sit down, Sally.
Take out your book, Sally.
Sing a song, Sally.
Take out two pencils, Sally.

Body and feelings (S. 7)
Zu 1.:
Circle Sally's ears.
Circle Sally's hands.
Circle Sally's eyes.
Circle Sally's nose.

Zu 2.:
Two little eyes to look around,
two little ears to hear each sound,
one little nose to smell what's sweet,
one little mouth that likes to eat.

Zu 3.:
Draw a sad face. Draw a happy face.

Toys (S. 8)
Zu 1.:
Colour the doll red.
Colour the ball green.
Colour the car blue.
Colour the train brown.
Colour the teddy bear yellow.

Zu 2.:
Circle the very big ball.
Circle the small book.
Circle the big tree.
Circle the small doll.

Zu 3.:
Draw one car.
Draw two balls.

Clothes (S. 9)
Zu 1.:
Hang up the clothes.
Number 1:
Hang up the woolly hat.
Number 2:
Hang up the socks.
Number 3:
Hang up the trousers.
Number 4:
Hang up the skirt.

Zu 2.:
Ellen is wearing a skirt, a T-shirt and socks.
Peter is wearing a pullover, trousers and a pair of shoes.

Zu 3.:
Draw a red skirt.
Draw blue trousers.
Draw a yellow woolly hat.

Animals (S. 10)
Zu 1.:
Colour the fish orange.
Colour the bird yellow.
Colour the dog black.
Colour the mouse grey.
Colour the cat brown.

Zu 2.:
Mum, can I have a dog, please?
No, it's too snappy.
Mum, can I have a pig, please?
Yes, you can.
Mum, can I have a cat, please?
No, it's too hairy.
Mum, can I have a mouse, please?
No, it's too little.
Mum, can I have a bird, please?
Yes, I like birds, too.

Zu 3.:
Number 1:
Phil: *My animal says blub, blub.*
Number 2:
Emily: *My animal says bow-wow.*
Number 3:
Eric: *My animal says chirp, chirp.*
Number 4:
Liz: *My animal says squeak, squeak.*

Fruit (S. 11)

Zu 1.:
Draw two apples.
Draw four cherries.
Draw one banana.

Zu 2.:
Phil: *In my basket is an apple, an orange and a pear.*
Susan: *In my basket are three cherries, two bananas and an apple.*

Zu 3.:
Number 1:
Pour the banana milk shake into your cup.
Number 2:
Cut the banana.
Number 3:
Wash your hands.
Number 4:
Peel the banana.

Family (S. 12)

Zu 1.:
Number 1:
You can see me with my brother.
Number 2:
You can see my mum and my dad.
Number 3:
You can see my mum and my sister.
Number 4:
You can see me with my family.

Zu 2.:
Daddy frog is singing a song.
Brother frog is jumping into the pond.
Sister frog is reading a book.
Baby frog is playing with a ball.
Mother frog is eating a banana.

Zu 3.:
Colour the big frog blue.
Colour the little fish red.
Colour the little bird yellow.

Sally's English Test 2
Texte zu den Hörverstehensaufgaben

At school (S. 15)
Zu 1.:
Number 1:
The book is under the schoolbag.
Number 2:
The glue stick is on the schoolbag.
Number 3:
The ruler is in the pencil case.
Number 4:
The rubber is on the book.

Zu 2.:
15 – 8 – 19 – 3 – 11 – 2 – 10 – 20

Body and clothes/ I'm Jumping Jack (S. 16)
Zu 1.:
Sally puts on her socks.
Sally puts on her gloves.
Sally puts on her trousers.
Sally puts on her woolly hat.

Zu 2.:
Number 1:
I'm raising my arms.
Number 2:
I'm lifting my leg.
Number 3:
I'm clapping my hands.
Number 4:
I'm standing still.

Hobbies (S. 18)
Zu 1.:
Number 1:
Sally is playing with a train.
Number 2:
Sally is inline skating.
Number 3:
Sally is playing with a doll.
Number 4:
Sally is jumping rope.
Number 5:
Sally is playing cards.
Number 6:
Sally is playing ball.

Zu 2.:
Colour three cards blue.
Colour one teddy bear brown.
Colour the train red.
Colour two ropes yellow.
Colour four balls green.

Zu 3.:
The ball is behind the tree.
The ball is in front of the tree.
The ball is next to the tree.

Vegetables (S. 20)
Zu 1.:
Emma: *Hi, I'm Emma. I like lettuce and cucumbers.*
Tom: *Hi, I'm Tom. And I like radishes and beans very much.*
Linda: *Hello, I'm Linda. I like carrots and I like cucumbers, too.*

Zu 2.:
In box number 1 there are tomatoes, lettuce and beans.
In box number 2 there are turnips, cucumbers and carrots.
In box number 3 there are beans, tomatoes and carrots.
In box number 4 there are radishes, cucumbers and lettuce.

Weather (S. 22)
Zu 1.:
Tom: *Hi, Grandma.*
Grandma: *Hello, Tom. How are you?*
Tom: *Fine. What's the weather like, Grandma?*
Grandma: *Oh, it's rainy. I can't go out in the garden.*

Helen: *Hi, Tom.*
Tom: *Hello, Helen. What are you doing?*
Helen: *I'm playing in the garden. It's sunny.*

Tom: *Hello, Grandpa.*
Grandpa: *Hello, my little boy.*
Tom: *How are you, Grandpa?*
Grandpa: *I'm fine. But it's very cold and it's snowy.*

Tom: *Good morning, Matt.*
Matt: *Good morning. Let's go inline skating. It's sunny outside.*

Zu 2.:
Number 1: Sally is playing in the garden. It's sunny.
Number 2: Suddenly the wind starts to blow. Sally's hat flies away.
Number 3: Here comes the rain.
Number 4: Sally gets all wet. "Oh no", says Sally and she runs into the house.

Farm animals (S. 24)

Zu 1.:
On the farm
there is an old lady.
Number 1:
The old lady swallows a duck.
Number 2:
The old lady swallows a horse.
Number 3:
The old lady swallows a pig.
Number 4:
The old lady swallows a sheep.

Zu 2.:
The pig under the table is brown.
The duck in the pond is yellow.
The hen on the house is red.
The horse in front of the tree is black.
The sheep next to the table is grey.

Seasons (S. 26)

Zu 1.:
Emma: *Hi, my name is Emma. My birthday's in spring. I like inline skating.*
Tom: *Hello, I'm Tom. My birthday's in winter. I've got a dog. His name is Toby.*
Linda: *Hi, my name is Linda. My birthday's in summer. I love ice cream.*
Bill: *Hi, my name is Bill. My birthday's in autumn. I'm 7 years old.*

Zu 2.:
Number 1: *I like summer and spring. I don't like autumn. It's too windy and rainy.*
Number 2: *I don't like autumn and summer. But I like snow in winter.*

Lernstandsbogen

Name: _____   Zusätzliche Beobachtungen: _____

Klasse: _____ Schuljahr: _____   _____

Hörverstehen	Datum	Gelingt sehr gut	Gelingt mit Hilfe	Hat noch Probleme	Bemerkungen
Kann den Inhalt von Geschichten/Texten erfassen					
Kann Schlüsselwörter in einer Geschichte/einem Text erkennen					
Kann auch unbekannte Wörter im Kontext erschließen					
Kann Arbeitsanweisungen verstehen und umsetzen					

Sprachproduktion	Datum	Gelingt in freier Reproduktion	Gelingt imitativ	Hat noch Probleme	Bemerkungen
Beherrscht die korrekte Aussprache					
Benutzt vorher geübte Redewendungen und Redemittel					
Kann Lieder und Reime mitsingen bzw. mitsprechen					

	Datum	Regelmäßig	Ab und zu	Nie	Bemerkungen
Zeigt eigenständige Versuche, die englische Sprache anzuwenden					

Leseverstehen	Datum	Gelingt ohne Hilfe	Gelingt mit Hilfe	Hat noch Probleme	Bemerkungen
Kann das Schriftbild einzelner Wörter erkennen und ihnen Bedeutung zuordnen					
Kann einfache, durch Piktogramme unterstützte Anweisungen umsetzen					

Schreiben	Datum	Gelingt ohne Hilfe	Gelingt mit Hilfe	Hat noch Probleme	Bemerkungen
Kann Wörter und einfache Wendungen schreiben					

Weitere mögliche Kriterien der Beobachtung:
- Interesse an der englischen Sprache
- Arbeitsverhalten (z. B. Heftführung)
- Selbsteinschätzung

Hinweise zur Überprüfung der Sprechfertigkeit

Mit den vier beiliegenden Bildkarten kann die Lehrkraft die Sprechfertigkeit der Kinder überprüfen. Die Kinder sollten einzeln getestet werden.
Unit- und themenübergreifend wird das Kind zum freien Sprechen angeregt: *Look at the picture.* Wenn sich das Kind nicht mehr äußert, kann die Lehrkraft gezielte Fragen zum Bild stellen und dabei ggf. auf bestimmte Bildausschnitte deuten.
Die Sprechfertigkeit kann in einem Sprachstandsbogen für jedes Kind dokumentiert werden (siehe Seite 38 und 39).

Bildkarte 1: Hello!
(Sally 1 bis Unit *Toys*)

mögliche Impulse:
What colour is/are …?
How many … (balls/books/…) can you see?
What number is it?
How does this child feel?
What are they doing?

Bildkarte 2: My family
(Sally 1 bis Unit *Family*)

mögliche Impulse:
What is (Daddy/the brother/…) doing?
What animals can you see?
How many (birds/oranges/…) can you see?
Who's playing ball?
Which fruit can you see?
What colour are the fruit?
Do you like …?
What's growing on the trees?
Which animals are in the picture?
What is the family doing?
What does the (pig/dog …) say?

Bildkarte 3: At school
(Sally 2 bis Unit *It's teatime*)

mögliche Impulse:
What is he/she doing?
What are the children doing?
What are they wearing?
Which clothes can you see?
Where is …?
What colour is …?
What is the teacher doing?
How many … can you see?

Bildkarte 4: In the garden
(Sally 2 bis Unit *Seasons*)

mögliche Impulse:
Which animals can you see?
Who's in the garden?
What are they doing?
Which vegetables are in the garden?
How many … can you see?
Which vegetables do you like?
What are the children doing?
What's the weather like?

Sprachstandsbogen

Bildkarte 1: Hello!	keine	wenige	einige	viele	Bemerkungen
Das Kind konnte weitgehend frei Szenen des Bildes beschreiben.					
Auf gezielte Nachfragen konnte das Kind Antworten geben.					
Die Antworten des Kindes waren ausschließlich Einwortsätze.					
Die Antworten des Kindes waren auch Mehrwortsätze.					
Das Kind verwendete Nomen.					
Das Kind verwendete Adjektive.					
Das Kind verwendete Verben.					
Das Kind verwendete Präpositionen.					
Zusätzliche Beobachtungspunkte, z. B. Aussprache: _____					

Bildkarte 2: My family	keine	wenige	einige	viele	Bemerkungen
Das Kind konnte weitgehend frei Szenen des Bildes beschreiben.					
Auf gezielte Nachfragen konnte das Kind Antworten geben.					
Die Antworten des Kindes waren ausschließlich Einwortsätze.					
Die Antworten des Kindes waren auch Mehrwortsätze.					
Das Kind verwendete Nomen.					
Das Kind verwendete Adjektive.					
Das Kind verwendete Verben.					
Das Kind verwendete Präpositionen.					
Zusätzliche Beobachtungspunkte, z. B. Aussprache: _____					

Bildkarte 3: At school	keine	wenige	einige	viele	Bemerkungen
Das Kind konnte weitgehend frei Szenen des Bildes beschreiben.					
Auf gezielte Nachfragen konnte das Kind Antworten geben.					
Die Antworten des Kindes waren ausschließlich Einwortsätze.					
Die Antworten des Kindes waren auch Mehrwortsätze.					
Das Kind verwendete Nomen.					
Das Kind verwendete Adjektive.					
Das Kind verwendete Verben.					
Das Kind verwendete Präpositionen.					
Zusätzliche Beobachtungspunkte, z. B. Aussprache:					

Bildkarte 4: In the garden	keine	wenige	einige	viele	Bemerkungen
Das Kind konnte weitgehend frei Szenen des Bildes beschreiben.					
Auf gezielte Nachfragen konnte das Kind Antworten geben.					
Die Antworten des Kindes waren ausschließlich Einwortsätze.					
Die Antworten des Kindes waren auch Mehrwortsätze.					
Das Kind verwendete Nomen.					
Das Kind verwendete Adjektive.					
Das Kind verwendete Verben.					
Das Kind verwendete Präpositionen.					
Zusätzliche Beobachtungspunkte, z. B. Aussprache:					

Inhalt der beiliegenden CD

Sally's English Test 1

Track

1	Colours and numbers (S. 5) – Aufgabe 1
2	Colours and numbers (S. 5) – Aufgabe 2
3	Colours and numbers (S. 5) – Aufgabe 3
4	My schoolbag (S. 6) – Aufgabe 1
5	My schoolbag (S. 6) – Aufgabe 2
6	My schoolbag (S. 6) – Aufgabe 3
7	Body and feelings (S. 7) – Aufgabe 1
8	Body and feelings (S. 7) – Aufgabe 2
9	Body and feelings (S. 7) – Aufgabe 3
10	Toys (S. 8) – Aufgabe 1
11	Toys (S. 8) – Aufgabe 2
12	Toys (S. 8) – Aufgabe 3
13	Clothes (S. 9) – Aufgabe 1
14	Clothes (S. 9) – Aufgabe 2
15	Clothes (S. 9) – Aufgabe 3
16	Animals (S. 10) – Aufgabe 1
17	Animals (S. 10) – Aufgabe 2
18	Animals (S. 10) – Aufgabe 3
19	Fruit (S. 11) – Aufgabe 1
20	Fruit (S. 11) – Aufgabe 2
21	Fruit (S. 11) – Aufgabe 3
22	Family (S. 12) – Aufgabe 1
23	Family (S. 12) – Aufgabe 2
24	Family (S. 12) – Aufgabe 3

Sally's English Test 2

Track

25	At school (S. 15) – Aufgabe 1
26	At school (S. 15) – Aufgabe 2
27	Body and clothes/ I'm Jumping Jack (S. 16) – Aufgabe 1
28	Body and clothes/ I'm Jumping Jack (S. 16) – Aufgabe 2
29	Hobbies (S. 18) – Aufgabe 1
30	Hobbies (S. 18) – Aufgabe 2
31	Hobbies (S. 18) – Aufgabe 3
32	Vegetables (S. 20) – Aufgabe 1
33	Vegetables (S. 20) – Aufgabe 2
34	Weather (S. 22) – Aufgabe 1
35	Weather (S. 22) – Aufgabe 2
36	Farm animals (S. 24) – Aufgabe 1
37	Farm animals (S. 24) – Aufgabe 2
38	Seasons (S. 26) – Aufgabe 1
39	Seasons (S. 26) – Aufgabe 2

Tonaufnahmen: Flödl, Ton-und Datenträger, Ziemetshausen
Sprecher: Andre Foster; David, Kerstin und Martin Ingram; Luca Italiano; Tom und Valerie James; Rachel und Robby Lindner